WHEN THE GROUND SHAKES

This book is dedicated to all children
who live in earthquake-prone areas.

AUTHORS Irit Almog & Shoshana Wheeler

INTERIOR ILLUSTRATOR David R. Aseraf

COVER ILLUSTRATOR Tim Kummerow

DESIGNER Yael Michelson

EDITOR Sharone Almog

www.children911resources.com
Children911Resources@gmail.com

Children 911 Resources
5308 Derry Avenue
Suite L 201
Agoura Hills CA 91301

WHEN THE GROUND SHAKES

WRITTEN BY IRIT ALMOG & SHOSHANA WHEELER
ILLUSTRATED BY DAVID R. ASERAF

CHILDREN 911 RESOURCES

EMPOWERING PARENTS FOR CHILDREN

INTRODUCTION
Dear Educator, Parent, Caregiver:

Preparing children for an unpredictable event, such as an earthquake, is one of the best ways to reduce trauma and maintain children's mental and emotional well-beings. We combined our experiences as a Marriage & Family Therapist and School Counselor to write this book, both specializing in work with young children for more than 20 years. Our first-hand experience helping children cope with traumas, including natural disasters, is what opened our eyes to the need for this type of self-help guidance book. This book was written to introduce the concept of an earthquake, and to provide children with tools to stay safe and cope during the event. There are books available that teach children what to do during an earthquake. The purpose of our book is to address children's emotional well-beings and to help reduce their anxiety and fear. Children learn through repetition. We recommend reading and practicing the skills introduced in this book on a regular basis. This book can also be used post-earthquake to help kids cope with their emotions and help them make sense of what has happened. When children know what to do, they are less likely to be scarred by the traumatic event.

We hope adults and children find this book informative and fun, even in the most stressful times.

Warmly,
Irit Almog & Shoshana Wheeler

"Even the most seasoned educators or parents of pre-school early elementary aged children will find much to learn from these two authors. Their book is a perfect resource for early care educators and parents looking for helpful information and methods to address children's emotional well-being affected by traumatic events, such as earthquakes. As a professional in the early care and education field, I can say this book is a true gift to all of us."

Jack Hinojosa
Chief Operations Officer
Child Development Resources of Ventura County, Inc

"When the Ground Shakes is an engaging, age-appropriate book for pre-schoolers and early elementary-aged children. The authors show children (and their parents) how to move their fear of the unknown into concrete, perhaps lifesaving, actions that will serve them well in any emergency situation. This gem of a book is a must for those who want to help our youngest children cope with the real trauma of earthquakes. All schools in California should take note of this book!"

Sheila Grady
Principal
Lupin Hill Elementary School

"A very informative and helpful book for elementary school students. Children of all ages will benefit from this book. With its repetitive practice of calming techniques students at school will feel more equipped to handle the scary feelings an earthquake can bring."

Lisa Hildebrand
Director of Education
Ventura Charter School of Arts & Global Education

Everybody likes to move their bodies.

We can shake our hands – Shake, Shake, Shake

We can shake our feet – Shake, Shake, Shake

We can shake our shoulders – Shake, Shake, Shake

We can shake our heads – Shake, Shake, Shake

We can shake our whole bodies – Shake, Shake, Shake

CDEFGHIJKLMNOPQRSTUVW

Shake, Shake, Shake

Do you know what else can shake?

Leaves on trees can shake.

Flowers can move and shake.

And sometimes, even the earth can shake.

When the earth shakes it is called an earthquake.

When the earth shakes, it is always a surprise.

We don't know when it is going to happen
because we can't see deep under the ground
where the shaking starts.

However, we can still be prepared for
when an earthquake happens.

It can be loud and noisy when the earth shakes. Earthquakes can set off car alarms, home alarms and even dogs may bark, but only for a short time. The good thing about an earthquake is that it doesn't last long. It usually lasts around 10 - 15 seconds.

Let's count 15 seconds out loud.

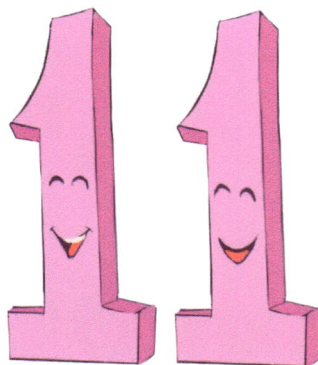

1 2 3 4

9 10 11 12

5 6 7 8

13 14 15

This is about how long an earthquake lasts.

The
shaking
is
over!

Most earthquakes last 10 - 15 seconds,
but some earthquakes can be longer.
If you have counted to 15 and the ground is still
shaking, it might be a longer earthquake.
To stay calm during a longer earthquake,
start singing your favorite songs.
Soon the shaking will be over.
No matter how long they last,
earthquakes always end.

It's a good idea to know which songs you will sing.
Practicing can help.

The earth can shake

chairs,
tables,
boOks,
beds,
Windows,
and even hOuses.

When everything is

shaking,
shaking,
shaking,

what can we do to be safe?

If you are in bed,

stay there and put a pillow over your head.

take a deep breath and count slowly.

1 2 3 4 5 6 7 8
9 10 11 12 13 14 15

If it is a little longer, take a deep breath and start

singing your favorite song.

Breathe and sing, breathe and sing until the shaking

stops. It may feel like a long time, but remember,

No matter how long the shaking lasts,

earthquakes always end.

1 2 3 4 5 6 7 8
9 10 11 12 13 14 15

If you are in the kitchen,
make sure to move away from the stove,
the refrigerator, and any shelves or cupboards!
We don't want a plate to
fall
on
your
head!

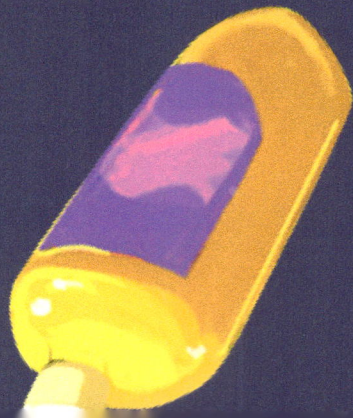

If you are in the car with mom, dad,
or another adult, they will pull over
to the side of the road and stop.
You will stay inside the car until the shaking is
over. While you are waiting, don't forget to take a
deep breath, and count. If the shaking lasts longer,
sing your favorite songs with everybody in the car.
Soon the shaking will stop.

When you are at school,
drop under a table or desk.
Cover your head with your hands
and **HOLD ON!**
Breathe, and count to 15;
1 2 3 4 5 6 7 8 9 10 11 12 13 14 15
Remember, if it is a little longer,
start singing your favorite songs.
Soon it will be over.

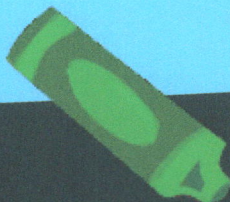

Even though you never know
when an earthquake is going to happen,
knowing what to do can make you feel safer.
So now, if we feel the ground shake,
what do we do to stay calm?
We

breathe,

count,

and

sing!

Soon it will be over.

1 2 3 4 5 6 7 8
9 10 11 12 13 14 15

FOLLOW UP
Dear Educator, Parent, Caregiver:

After reading this book to your child, your next step is to utilize our follow-up workbook, which can be purchased separately.

INTRODUCTION TO WORKBOOK
Children learn about the world from eductors, parents, and caregivers. In every moment, we are the ones who teach our children how to react to the world around them and to life's circumstances through our reactions and emotional states of being. During a crisis or disaster, children will have emotional reactions.

Our mission and hope is that through these activities you will gain an understanding of what a child may feel in a crisis or catastrophic event and how to help your child/student best cope under these circumstances. Young children may not have words to express their fear and anxiety.
Our activities provide outlets for such children. In the event of a crisis we want

you, the parent/caregiver/teacher to be the child's emotional coach, and provide guidance with our tools. We want to emphasize the importance of practicing these games and exercises, as repetition is fundamental to learning.

For example, through daily practice of learning letters and sounds, children learn to read and write. We hope you have fun practicing these activities, so that in the event of a crisis, your children/students will be prepared and know how to respond. It is equally as important to practice and play these activities after a crisis to assist them in processing the experience.

Warmly,
Irit Almog & Shoshana Wheeler

Earthquake Kit for Kids

Ten Essential items in the event of an earthquake:

1. Whistle

2. Flashlight

3. Water

4. Energy Bar

5. Baggie with band-aids

6. Glasses (if you wear them)

7. Your favorite toy or stuffed animal

8. Crayons or markers

9. Change of clothes

10. "When The Ground Shakes" workbook

Parents, this emergency kit is for your child. If there is something pertaining to him/her that you think he/she should have, please add it to the list. For a detailed family Earthquake Preparedness Kit, go online to:
www.FEMA.gov/disaster.

www.ingramcontent.com/pod-product-compliance
Lightning Source LLC
Chambersburg PA
CBHW060815090426

42737CB00002B/74